THE WORLD
OF THE KENNEDY WOMEN

The World of The Kennedy Women

Profiles in Grace and Courage

Edited by Lois Daniel

Illustrated by Bernard Fuchs

HALLMARK EDITIONS

The Kennedy women
are all feminine,
but it is obvious that they are feminine
in the modern, horseback-riding,
tennis-playing fashion.
None of them is a humble housewife.
They are independent but considerate,
efficient as a matter of course
but careless of praise,
ambitious but not personally so.
They are team workers,
and the entire family ...
is the team.

Pearl S. Buck

It can be said that the entire Kennedy family
was founded on the courage of a woman.
Had Rose Fitzgerald not had the strength and
independence of spirit to marry
Joseph P. Kennedy over the protests of her
powerful father, the Kennedy family,
as we know it, would not have emerged to leave
its indelible mark on the United States
and on the world:

This beautiful girl learned early to accept and deal with fate as it attacked. She was Irish and in conservative old Boston society the Irish were intruders. When Rose applied for membership to the Junior League, she was refused. Did she accept the refusal meekly? She did not. She formed her own organization, the Ace of Clubs, which became as exclusive as the Junior League. She began the Travel Club, she became president of the Lenox Club and belonged to other organizations in whose work she was interested. Never were the clubs purely social. She had a serious depth in her nature, and if her interest were to be caught and held, it must be by some useful purpose. She was therefore an interesting combination of her humor-loving father and her quiet, home-loving mother.

With all this, she was also glamorous, and many men loved her. Her debut into Irish society was talked about as an affair unique in its glitter, with four hundred and fifty of Boston's rich young men and women. Among the men who, it was said, asked to marry her was the Englishman Sir Thomas Lipton, yachtsman, tea merchant, and her father's friend. . . .

She chose fiery, red-haired Joseph P. Kennedy, a youthful banker who stood at the start of an enormously successful financial career. He had already gained control of the Columbia Trust Company in East Boston and, at twenty-five, had become the youngest bank president in Massachusetts.

In spite of this he was no favorite of her father, who opposed the marriage. When Joe put the engagement ring on her finger, he did so as they stood together on the sidewalk. Her father, Honey Fitz, would not let him into the house.

Three decades after she defied her father by
marrying Joseph P. Kennedy, Rose Fitzgerald
Kennedy was to find herself in the position
of a parent disapproving of her own daughter's
marriage. Kathleen, her eldest daughter,
proved to be her mother's child when she, too,
had the courage to marry the man she loved
against the wishes of her parents:

Kathleen had first met William John Robert Cavendish, the Marquess of Hartington, in 1938 at a garden party near London. She was then seventeen, the daughter of the new American Ambassador, and Billy Hartington, as the young lord's friends called him, was nineteen. He had been mentioned as an eligible suitor for the Crown Princess. . . .

The Cavendishes had been outstanding members of the British nobility since 1366. When Henry the Eighth broke up the monasteries and established the Protestant Church of England, a large share of the Catholic lands was given to . . . Sir William Cavendish. Not only had the family been unswervingly Protestant ever since, but Billy's father, the tenth Duke of Devonshire, was head of the Freemasons. . . .

The staunchly Catholic Kennedys, especially Rose, were as dismayed by the religious difference as the Cavendishes. Nobody in her family was more troubled than Kathleen herself. An unusually devout girl, educated in Sacred Heart convent schools in Connecticut and France, her Catholicism was vital to her. She discussed her problem with the Apostolic Delegate in London and tried at length to persuade Lord Hartington to agree to allow their children to be brought up as Catholics. With such an agreement, she could have obtained a dispensation permitting her marriage to the non-Catholic lord to be performed by a Catholic priest. As the next Duke of Devonshire, Lord Hartington felt an obligation to refuse to enter such an agreement. . . . The only thing left was a civil ceremony performed by a registrar, the British equivalent of an American justice of the peace, which Kathleen agreed to . . . as a final, desperate resort. . . .

The Marquess and the Marchioness were able to live together for only a little more than a month in their apartment at 4 Smith Square in the Westminster section of London. Then he went into combat in France with his Guards regiment and she went to the United States, planning to stay with her family for the duration of the war.

*Only a few months after her marriage
and three weeks after the death of her beloved
brother Joe, Kathleen received word that
her husband had been killed in action:*

In a plane provided by the British government, she flew at once to be with the parents of the husband she had scarcely known; they embraced her as a daughter. Thereafter, Kathleen remained in England, and made a long spiritual retreat. In a letter to a friend some time after her husband's death, she expressed the resignation born of the faith that had sustained her. "I guess God has taken care of the problem in His own way, hasn't He?"

In 1944, the Duchess of Devonshire wrote a letter to Rose Kennedy that began: "I want to tell you of the joy that Kathleen brought into my son's life...." For four years, Kathleen separated herself from her family, becoming more a Cavendish than a Kennedy. Then, early in May, 1948, Kathleen and her father, who was in Paris, made plans to vacation together on the Riviera. A friend in London, Earl Fitzwilliam, a wealthy thirty-eight-year-old peer, was flying to Cannes and invited her to join him aboard his small chartered plane. Flying at night in rain and fog, the plane smashed into the side of a peak in the mountains of the Ardéche. Kathleen, Fitzwilliam, and the two crew members were killed instantly.

Joe Kennedy flew from Paris to Lyon, then hurried to the small village of Privas, in the Rhone Valley. Informed that his daughter's passport had been found in the wreckage, he said he would not give up hope that there was some mistake. Grief-stricken, he watched as his beloved "Kick's" body was brought down from the mountainside in a peasant's cart. The twenty-eight-year-old Kathleen was buried, next to her husband, in the cemetery at Chatsworth, Derbyshire.

Jacqueline describes her on-again, off-again courtship with young John Kennedy:

It was a very spasmodic courtship. We didn't see each other for six months, because I went to Europe again, and Jack began his summer and fall campaigning in Massachusetts. Then came six months when we were both back. Jack was in Congress, and I was in my last year at George Washington University. But it was still spasmodic, because he spent half of each week in Massachusetts. He'd call me from some oyster bar up there, with a great clinking of coins, to ask me out to the movies the following Wednesday in Washington. He loved Westerns and Civil War pictures. He was not the candy-and-flowers type, so every now and then he'd give me a book. He gave me *The Raven*, which is the life of Sam Houston, and also *Pilgrim's Way* by John Buchan.

13

She's poetic, whimsical,
provocative, independent,
and yet very feminine.
Jackie has always kept
her own identity
and been different.
That's important
in a woman.

Robert Kennedy

*Jacqueline realized soon after her marriage
that the Kennedys never lost either a son or
daughter to marriage. Instead, they absorbed
the new in-law into their closely knit clan.
In spite of almost overwhelming odds,
Jacqueline managed to retain her identity
and even to make the Kennedys like it:*

Easily the most dazzling Kennedy in-law, and perhaps the most challenging to the head of the family, was Jack's wife, the intelligent and strong-willed former Jacqueline Lee Bouvier. The daughter of a wealthy East Hampton, Long Island, stockbroker, she was a regally poised member of America's untitled aristocracy. Hers was the small, rigorously selective world of hunt meets, country estates, and inherited Republican loyalties, a world the elder Kennedy knew well but one in which he was not at ease. When the young Kennedys had been loudly debating political questions at the Hyannis Port dinner table, Jacqueline and her parents had been conversing by candlelight in elegant French. When she made her debut at Newport, the ecstatic society columnist "Cholly Knickerbocker" dubbed her "Queen Deb of the Year." Newport also was the scene of her wedding to Jack in September, 1953, an extravaganza attended by seven hundred guests and almost disrupted by a mob of three thousand spectators.

As a bride, Jackie shrank from the compulsive athleticism and togetherness of the Kennedy clan. ("Just watching them wore me out," she said of her hyperactive in-laws.) After injuring an ankle trying to play touch football, she withdrew from the family scrimmages. She firmly refused to attend the nightly family dinners at her father-in-law's house. "Once a week is great," she told her husband. "Not every night." The inevitable head-on collision with the elder Kennedy came one day in Palm Beach when she was fifteen minutes late to lunch. "That can be fatal with Joe when he's in one of his Emperor Augustus moods," recalled a family friend who witnessed the scene. "So when she came in, he started to give her the needle, but she gave it right back. Old Joe has a lot of old-fashioned slang phrases, so Jackie told him: 'You ought to write a series of grandfather stories for children, like 'The Duck With Moxie,' and 'The Donkey Who Couldn't Fight His Way Out of a Telephone Booth.' When she said this, the old man was silent for a minute. Then he broke into a roar of laughter."

*Nine months after he became
Attorney General, Robert F. Kennedy
was asked what he considered the major
achievement of his life. He was, at the moment,
nibbling a piece of toast and sipping a glass
of milk before rushing to the White House.
Ethel Kennedy sat across an oval mahogany
table from her husband, and three of the
little Kennedys romped through the gracious
dining room at Hickory Hill:*

When the question was asked by a breakfast guest, the Attorney General dropped his head, fixed his eyes on the worn oak flooring and pondered fifty, possibly sixty seconds. His slow and almost somber deliberation prompted Ethel to shoot a blithe verbal dart across the table. "That quick mind!" she quipped.

The Attorney General pondered on, recalling the senatorial and presidential elections he helped his brother to win, the success he had had in spotlighting corruption in the union movement, the writing of his book *The Enemy Within*, his handling of difficult problems at the Department of Justice. Then abruptly he was transformed into a happy leprechaun. His face lit up and wrinkled up at the same moment, like

that of a child who has for the first time seen and touched a newborn puppy. He flashed a smile across the table at his wife and, in a voice filled with playful mockery, declared triumphantly: "Marrying Ethel."

Ethel Kennedy accepted the tribute in the manner in which it was paid—with laughter— and responded: "It certainly took you long enough to decide."

An exciting hoarse voice,
a shriek, a peal of screaming laughter,
the flash of shirt-tails,
a tousled brown head — Ethel!
Her face is at one moment
a picture of utter guilelessness
and at the next alive with mischief. . . .
The 49ers
didn't have to search very far
to find in Ethel
a heart of gold.

The 1949 *Tower*
Yearbook of Manhattanville College
of the Sacred Heart

*Jean Kennedy's marriage to Stephen Smith
had her parents' enthusiastic approval. It is a
marriage which has proved to be a major
blessing to the Kennedy family:*

Stephen Smith has a quiet strength of his own. His family "had money" long before the Kennedys knew the advantages of wealth. Without losing his own personality, he has used his talents and experience to serve the Kennedy family. . . .

He was a young business executive, already successful, when he married Jean Kennedy in 1956. Jean Smith, blue-eyed and dark-haired, is the least political of the Kennedy women, and enjoys her home and its privacy. She is a good mother to her children and a good wife to her extremely intelligent young husband — so shrewd a business brain, by the way, that a year after his marriage his father-in-law invited him to manage and expand the Kennedy oil interests. Now he manages the Kennedy portfolio of investments of more than three hundred million dollars, which he charmingly refuses to discuss.

He fits well into the Kennedy family, for he is also an excellent athlete, admitted even by the

Patricia

Jean

family to be the best all-around sportsman of them all, in golf, tennis, skiing, and even touch football!

When Patricia married actor Peter Lawford, Joseph Kennedy made no attempt to conceal his displeasure:

The bride's bouquet at Eunice's wedding reception on the Starlight Roof of the Waldorf Astoria was caught by Patricia, the next daughter in line, and probably the best looking of the girls, as well as the tallest and the family's best golfer with the exception of the Ambassador himself. The following winter at Palm Beach Pat met Peter Lawford, the British-born Hollywood movie star. Lawford soon proposed, but Pat was determined not to be rushed into marriage. She was planning a trip around the world with a girl friend from Boston and she decided to delay a definite answer to

Lawford until the journey was over. Saying good-bye to Peter in San Francisco, she warned him that she would not be seeing him again for six months. She managed to get as far as Tokyo. There she realized that going on to India, the Middle East and Europe would be unbearable. With hurried apologies to her traveling companion, Pat caught the next plane back to California where Lawford was waiting for her when she landed. They decided that they would break the news to the Ambassador right away. Joe was not overjoyed at the prospect of having a Hollywood personality as a member of his family. Pat's father is reported to have said to Lawford, "If there's anything I think I'd hate as a son-in-law, it's an actor, and if there's anything I think I'd hate worse than an actor as a son-in-law, it's an English actor." Lawford, a likeable and casual fellow, not at all in awe of the dynamic Kennedy men, was not a bit perturbed by the Ambassador.

Although two of his daughters married
without their father's blessing, Eunice could
hardly have chosen a man who would
please Joseph Kennedy more:

Eunice's husband, Sargent Shriver, was bound closely to the family even before marriage, serving first as assistant manager of the Merchandise Mart (the Chicago enterprise owned by the Kennedys) and later going to Washington at her father's suggestion, to assist Eunice with her study of Juvenile Delinquency. Their engagement came as no surprise to Kennedy, although he vehemently denied that he had played matchmaker.

Each member of the Kennedy family
has his own sphere of family responsibility.
Eunice Kennedy Shriver has represented
the family ably:

She is the most typical of the Kennedy women and one who, had she been born a generation or two later, would certainly have found politics her field. . . .

The Kennedy women who have married have not made easy wives. Their husbands have had to remain strong men. Sargent Shriver, seemingly so easygoing, seemingly so casual that he recently forgot or apparently forgot an important ambassadorial reception in our own embassy in Paris, is only apparently easygoing and casual. He wins his battles by his own methods. To see him with Eunice . . . is to learn how he does it. Obviously he loves her, obviously he understands her, he is always courteous, a gentleman born, always fair, always ready to hear her arguments, and yet one knows that his decisions are his own. He is pleasantly invincible.

There is an air of perfect understanding between the Shrivers, each allowing the other to speak without interruptions — no slight accomplishment for American men and their wives. . . . Between Eunice and her husband . . . there is mutual consideration and respect.

Eunice Shriver . . . hardworking,
brilliantly intelligent,
genuinely idealistic,
she is at the same time feminine.
Her slender frame is taut
as a coiled spring,
time is always too short
for her many activities,
her life is planned and has to be. . . .
She is an affectionate mother,
a devoted wife
but one with her own work
for which she is responsible.
She is more than competent
in her many roles.

Pearl S. Buck

*Throughout their years of marriage, both
John and Jacqueline Kennedy were plagued
by illness. It was during John's extended
hospitalization soon after their marriage that
he conceived of and wrote* Profiles in Courage.
*As Mary Van Rensselaer Thayer points out,
he couldn't have done it without the help
of his devoted wife:*

Down in Palm Beach, the senator found time in
bed hanging heavy. He commenced writing and
painting. A year or so
before he had read the
story of Kansas Sena-
tor Edmund Ross, a
promising young man serving his first senatorial
term who deliberately committed political sui-
cide by voting, against powerful pressures, ac-
cording to the dictates of his judgment for what
he considered "the highest good of the country."
His single vote prevented President Andrew
Johnson from being unjustly convicted.

Ross's courageous, almost-forgotten act in-
trigued the senator, and from it stemmed his
idea of discovering other such incidents and
gathering them into a book. So he cranked up his
hospital bed, asked the Library of Congress to
express him innumerable books and went to

work. He found seven other senators whom he five-starred for their political courage, and a handful of others, brave, but less conspicuously so. These true tales were melded together, interpreted by the senator and rounded out with his own personal philosophy of politics and courage. The result, *Profiles in Courage*, was a best seller and Pulitzer-prize winner.

Profiles in Courage couldn't have happened without Jacqueline. She encouraged her husband, read to him, carried out independent research and, on lined yellow copy paper, wrote down parts of the book. Her husband, listing thank-you credits in the preface, concluded: "This book would not have been possible without the encouragement, assistance and criticisms offered from the very beginning by my wife, Jacqueline, whose help during all the days of my convalescence I cannot ever adequately acknowledge."

Jackie possessed . . .
the most important quality —
complete loyalty to Jack.

Igor Cassini

It was not in the stars for that pair
to sink gently into each other's arms
in a soft corner,
murmuring a note of music
in perfect key.
It seems to have been a good, fair,
running argument in the open —
heaven knows there was no place
for them to hide;
eyes, ears and cameras were everywhere
by then — and we know
that things were coming out well.
We could see it in their expressions
as time ran on,

and the cameras intercepted
their glances at each other,
saw them off guard
at moments of greeting, of parting,
their clasped hands
as they came out of the hospital
after Patrick was born—
anybody could see that the marriage
was growing
into something grand and final,
fateful and tragic,
with birth and death and love in it
at every step.

Katherine Anne Porter

*When Joan Kennedy was asked if there
were any myths about herself that she would
like to correct, she answered, "Well, how would
you like to be thought of as just a sexy blonde?"
There are many incidents in Joan's life
which prove she is a person of intelligence,
strength and integrity. Her performance in
her husband's 1964 campaign is only one
example of Joan's abilities:*

Of all the Kennedy women, Joan is the most
polished campaigner. When Ted first ran for the
Senate in 1962, she helped him
in the usual wifely fashion,
appearing at ladies' lunches
and teas. But in 1964, when the
plane crash left her husband totally incapacita-
ted for months, it was Joan, just three weeks out
of the hospital after a miscarriage, who took his
place on the campaign trail. Says longtime Kennedy aide Eddie Martin, "Suddenly, Joan found
herself in the unique (for her) role of campaign
manager. Beginning with the simple fact that
she wasn't a professional politician or public
speaker, it was a formidable task. Yet most of the
time she spoke extemporaneously. Her prefer-
ence is to be a housewife, but her general attitude
is anything to help Ted . . . ."

Sally Fitzgerald, a Boston cousin-in-law and seasoned politico, became Joan's campaign companion. Here Sally tells about their part in the so-called "Kennedy Machine":

We laugh about it. Joan had this little brown rented car — she called it the Army car — the cheapest model made. We went to all the hick places that Ted would've skipped, and we did a *lot* of ringing of doorbells. That's where Joan loves campaigning — asking women about the children, the home. While Ted would've been out for the big handshakes, Joan was out getting the pulse of what the women wanted out of Ted and for their children.

Ethel talking about her sister-in-law Joan:

There isn't a toenail that isn't absolutely gorgeous, and she is as beautiful on the inside as she is on the outside.

When John F. Kennedy was running
for Congress in 1946, his campaign manager
decided that the campaign needed an extra
touch of excitement and asked if Jack's mother
would enter the campaign and give a series
of speeches at rallies in Boston. At first
Ambassador Kennedy was dubious. Joseph
McCarthy, author of The Remarkable Kennedys,
tells how it turned out:

The Ambassador frowned on the proposal. "But she's a grandmother," he objected.

"She's also a Gold Star mother, the mother of a Congressman and a war hero, the beautiful wife of Ambassador Joseph P. Kennedy and the daughter of John F. Fitzgerald — which means that she's hot stuff in Boston," Powers told him. "I need her and I've got to have her."

Rose Kennedy toured the city with Powers, changing in her car from the simple wraparound skirt and blouse that she wore at union halls and street corner meetings in tenement districts to the costly cocktail dress that she displayed with jewelry at formal hotel dinners. "Rose wowed them everywhere," Powers recalled recently. "She greeted the Italians in the North End with a few words of Italian and told them how she grew up in their neighborhood. In Dorchester, she talked about her days in Dorchester High School. She showed them the card index file she kept when her kids were little to keep track of the vaccinations and medical treatments and dental work. At a high-toned gathering of women, she'd talk for a few minutes about Jack and then she'd say, 'Now let me tell you about the new dresses I saw in Paris last month.' They loved her. . . ."

You just keep busy.
Some people get bored, and are boring.
You keep interested in other people
and in different activities.
I've always had a mind
that was probing and curious
and I've had the opportunity
to use it.

Rose Kennedy

Ethel Kennedy was totally devoted to her husband. Lester David tells this story:

Upon being named attorney general, RFK ordered FBI Director J. Edgar Hoover to funnel more agents into the fight against crime and fewer into the hunt for Communists. Hoover resented being told what to do, even by a man who was technically his boss, and a deep freeze developed between the two. One who rallied to Kennedy's side in the internal tug-of-war, thereby also calling down Hoover's wrath, was William Parker, the police chief of Los Angeles. Ethel, fuming at Hoover because he opposed Bobby, went to the FBI headquarters in the Department of Justice building and deposited a terse "suggestion" in the director's personal suggestion box. It read:

"Parker for FBI Director —

(Signed) Ethel Kennedy."

It was an extraordinary relationship. With Ethel and Bobby, everything just clicked all the way.

Ted Kennedy

So completely did Ethel enter into the life
of her husband's family, that she might
have been born a Kennedy:

Ethel long ago became accustomed to combining their public and family lives; in 1952, during John F. Kennedy's first senatorial campaign, she made a speech for her brother-in-law in Fall River, Mass., then drove directly to Boston where, before dawn, she gave birth to her first son, Joseph P. Kennedy III.

Bobby was a lonely,
very sensitive and unfulfilled youngster.
He met Ethel,
and all the love and appreciation
for which she seemed to have
an infinite capacity
came pouring down on him.
How he blossomed.

Eunice Kennedy Shriver

Jacqueline Kennedy's perception, finesse and innate good taste often made it possible for her to make a unique and highly valuable contribution to her husband's campaign. Kennedy friend Paul Fay describes one particular trip to Milwaukee where Jacqueline saved the day:

The hall, which could comfortably accommodate about fifteen hundred, was jam-packed with about three thousand people. Although it was pleasantly cool outside, the overcrowding and lack of air conditioning forced the temperature up into the nineties. At about 8:10 all the people who were to appear on the program except Jack and Jacqueline filed up on the stage.

Congressman Clem Zablocki announced: "Senator and Mrs. Kennedy will be a little late. Let's sing a few songs to give them a real Polish-American greeting when they arrive."

Clem was able to keep them singing for about twenty minutes, but the heat and the waiting soon took their toll. The crowd, having spent more than an hour waiting to get into the hall, now stood and sat in almost sullen silence.

Finally, about ten minutes before nine, the Senator and Jacqueline arrived to polite, subdued applause. Clem Zablocki said, "There was a mix-up in the schedule. The Senator had been told we were about five minutes from his headquarters instead of forty-five minutes." But the excuse fell on deaf ears. Clem then introduced Jacqueline. In her soft voice, she said simply, "We're terribly sorry to have kept you waiting so long when you'd been so nice to come. With so much to do in a campaign, it's a wonder that more mistakes aren't made which inconvenience people who are so kind and thoughtful as to encourage the candidate."

You could feel the tensions in the room running away, like a receding wave.

"I have great respect and affection for the Polish people; besides, my sister is married to a Pole," Jacqueline continued. Then in perfect Polish she stated, "Poland will live forever," and sat down.

The crowd burst into cheering and unashamed weeping.

Jack turned . . . and said, "How would you like to try and follow that?"

Thanks to a very lovely young lady the Polish vote . . . was saved for the Senator from Massachusetts.

President John Kennedy speaking
to members of the Paris press:

I do not think it altogether inappropriate for me to introduce myself. I am the man who accompanied Jacqueline Kennedy to Paris.

When asked to list his wife's
greatest contributions as First Lady,
John F. Kennedy replied:

Her emphasis on creative fields, her concentration on giving historical meaning to the White House furnishings, her success as an ambassador on the trips she has made with me abroad. And by carrying out her primary responsibility to back up her husband and care for her children well, she is doing her real job as a woman.

Everything centered around Jack.

Jacqueline Kennedy

Besides being good wives and campaign helpers, the Kennedy women are also credited with being excellent mothers — not an easy job with all the publicity surrounding them and their children. One of Rose Kennedy's friends says this about her:

I never saw a mother with such devotion to her children. When they had the house in Bronxville decorated by Elsie De Wolfe, Rose's room was furnished with pieces that had a very beautiful but very delicate . . . silk upholstery. Rose took one look at it and had it covered up immediately with rough, hard slip covers. She said the room was no good to her unless the smaller children could play in it with her. This great closeness that the Kennedys have as a family unit is entirely due to Rose.

Having a large family
is a more interesting experience
than any other that I know
and it ought to be viewed that way.
It's quite a challenge.
Children are interesting.
No two of them are alike.
You have to tend to the roots
as well as the stems
and slowly and carefully plant ideas
and concepts of right and wrong,
religion and social implications
and applications.
I always felt that if the older children
are brought up right,
the younger ones
will follow their lead.

Rose Kennedy

Ethel Kennedy's role as a mother has been a joyous one. Writer Pete Hamill describes a particular day when he and Senator Kennedy arrived at Hickory Hill:

Suddenly there was a loud crash and a sliding, scratching noise and the sound of running feet. We had obviously strolled into ambush country. There were dogs and kids everywhere: sniffing dogs and leaping kids, barking dogs and barking kids, big kids, little kids, kids grabbing Kennedy by the legs and lapels and the necktie. There was mad laughter and raucous squealing, and then two kids (male) had their hands up and were sparring with each other, while a great black Newfoundland dog named Brumus leaped between them. Kennedy said, "Hold it, there'll be none of that." And standing against the wall, literally convulsed with laughter, was Ethel. . . .

That's the thing that bothers people about Ethel Kennedy. Nobody is supposed really to *enjoy* children. If you have two or three children, you are supposed to despise the noisy dwarfs for intruding on your privacy. But Ethel Kennedy has *ten* kids. Why should she look as if she's having the time of her life . . . ?

Historian and White House advisor
Arthur M. Schlesinger, Jr., knew
the Kennedys well. Here he recalls
Jacqueline's abilities as a mother:

Jacqueline was determined that the children lead as normal lives as possible. This was not an easy goal for the young children of a President, but she did her best, arranging the White House nursery school where they could fraternize with their contemporaries, and taking them off in her blue Pontiac station wagon on quiet expeditions to shops or parks. On Halloween evening in 1962, the doorbell rang at my house in Georgetown. When my fourteen-year-old daughter opened the door to the trick-or-treaters, she found a collection of small hobgoblins leaping up and down. One seemed particularly eager to have her basket filled with goodies. After a moment a masked mother in the background called out that it was time to go to their next house. Christina suddenly recognized the voice. It was, of course, Jackie, and the excited little girl was Caroline out with her cousins. They had just rung Joe Alsop's bell; Dean Acheson was the next stop.

I guess lots of mothers
would say I'm too permissive
and too easy with the children . . .
but I just don't believe
a child's world should be
entirely full of 'don'ts.'
We think it's possible
to have discipline
and still give the children independence
without spoiling them. . . .

Ethel Kennedy

People have too many theories
about rearing children.
I believe simply in love,
security and discipline.

Jacqueline Kennedy

Immediately following the tragic death of President John F. Kennedy, his widow presented to the world a new profile in courage. Only later did she reveal her feelings in the following tribute:

It is nearly a year since he has been gone.

On so many days — his birthday, an anniversary, watching his children running to the sea — I have thought, "But this day last year was his last to see that." He was so full of love ... on all those days. He seems so vulnerable now, when you think that each one was a last time.

Soon the final day will come around again — as ... it did last year. But expected this time.

It will find some of us different people than we were a year ago. Learning to accept what was unthinkable when he was alive changes you.

I don't think there is any consolation. What was lost cannot be replaced.

Someone who loved President Kennedy, but who had never known him, wrote to me this winter: "The hero comes when he is needed. When our belief gets pale and weak, there comes a man out of that need who is shining—and everyone living reflects a little of that light — and stores some up against the time when he is gone."

Now I think that I should have known that he was magic all along. I did know it — but I should have guessed it could not last. I should have known that it was asking too much to dream that I might have grown old with him and see our children grow up together.

So now he is a legend when he would have preferred to be a man. I must believe that he does not share our suffering now. I think for him — at least he will never know whatever sadness might have lain ahead. He knew such a share of it in his life that it always made you so happy whenever you saw him enjoying himself. But now he will never know more — not age, nor stagnation, nor despair, nor crippling illness, nor loss of any more people he loved. His high noon kept all the freshness of the morning — and he died then, never knowing disillusionment.

". . . he has gone . . .
Among the radiant, ever venturing on,
Somewhere, with morning, as such spirits will."

He is free and we must live. Those who love him must know that "the death you have dealt is more than the death which has swallowed you."

Ethel Kennedy once remarked that "laughter is better than tears." These words might well be the motto by which Ethel has lived since the death of her husband. She has been determined to carry on courageously and without self-pity:

Never was there a more unlikely candidate for somber widowhood than Ethel Skakel Kennedy.

She has long been the eternal child of the Kennedy clan, bubbly and bouncy, irrepressibly vital and irresistibly friendly, a puckish foe of the false and the pompous, always loving and loyal to her husband, earnestly compassionate about animals, incessantly searching out joy — an authentic blithe spirit even in prolific motherhood. She was the one who could shepherd a vast and volatile brood of ten with the same wide-eyed zest that was visible when she was snagging a pass at touch football or riding a careening raft in and out of lethal rapids or zigzagging down the ski slopes. With the Kennedy family, Ethel was always the one who hurled herself impulsively into life as though it were indeed one big ball, or at the very least a romping surprise party to be relished with all the zest and gaiety that one could get and give.

"Laughter," she said, "is better than tears."

And for Ethel, a life of exuberant action was much better than one of morbid introspection. In Bobby's family, tragedies have been no less hers, too, for she was a totally married woman. Yet no anguish ever seemed to diminish her spirit.

Intimates hand Ethel the lioness's share of credit for retrieving her husband from the consuming spiral of melancholy following his brother's assassination. "Without her," a friend said, "Bobby might well have gone off the deep end." And sure enough, it was Ethel herself who elected to move about the plane that carried her own dead husband to New York in an effort to cheer up the . . . band of friends on board . . . .

And just as she has always been quick to offer compassion to others . . . she has always been free about admitting when she needed it herself. When making airplane landings, which she hated, she would unblushingly call for Bobby. "Would you mind getting my husband back here," she said as the plane approached one recent campaign stop. "He always holds my hand."

When the Presidential jet set down in New York after the flight from Los Angeles, the wiry, tanned little woman emerged with the casket —

holding nobody's hand. She moved unpausing...
past friends and strangers with a taut, flinch-
less mask that gave way neither at St. Patrick's
nor later at Arlington. She stood with invincible
composure, unapproachable it seemed, an apos-
tle of life at the rites of death.

She had always said she would take "whatever comes" in numbers of children. Providen-
tially, even at the time of death, life thrived in
her. Ethel Kennedy was carrying her eleventh
child — due seven months after its father's
death.

Ethel has no idea
how much her strength
and her own warmth
and goodwill have meant to others,
how much these things have meant
to the children,
how much she has helped them
and the Kennedy family.

Ted Kennedy

*Her son Jack called Rose Kennedy "the very
glue that held the Kennedys together." Here
author Sylvia Wright describes the spirit
and character of the Kennedy clan's
courageous matriarch:*

She keeps about her, as she always has in the big,
airy old house in Hyannis Port, her paintings,
her flowers, her portraits of
those giants her menfolk. All of
these are touchstones to a past
at once glorious and tragic —
interwoven, now, with her nation's history.
Many people might have tried to shut away all
memory of those sad events, and they marvel
that she has not. . . . At 80, she sits pert and smil-
ing at her polished concert grand and belts out
Sweet Adeline, her father's campaign song, just
as she did back in the 1900s when "Honey
Fitz" was politicking his way into legend. By
the time she was 15, she was already an accom-
plished christener of ships and shaker of hands,
but, she decided, "Pink teas bore me." While
her men — husband Joe, sons Joe Jr., John,
Robert and Edward — were becoming rich and
famous and powerful, and her daughters person-
ages in their own right, Rose never allowed herself to remain a mere adornment. She was, said

Jack, the very glue that held the Kennedys together. "I don't think I know anyone who has more courage than my wife," said old Joe once. "In all the years that we have been married, I have never heard her complain. Never. Not even once."

God will not give us a cross
heavier than we can bear.
Either you survive or you succumb.
If you survive,
you profit by the experience.
You understand the tragedies
of other people's lives.
You're more sympathetic
and a broader person.

Rose Kennedy

EPILOGUE:

The little girl who clomped about the White House in her mother's shoes and who, when asked by a reporter what her father was doing, replied, "Nothing, just sitting upstairs with his socks off," is now old enough to be considered a Kennedy woman.

When magazine writer Liz Smith began working on a story about Caroline Kennedy, her friends asked, "What is there to say about a thirteen-year-old kid?"

The answer is reflected in the joy of Caroline's voluminous and delightful preassassination press clips . . . in the tragedy of those two incredible deaths and funerals. This child has had outpourings of exotic gifts from heads of state and world leaders that must have forever ruined Christmas for her . . . she has talked with kings and prime ministers . . . she has been beset by photographers, strangers, maniacs on the street, autograph-seekers who wanted the mere mark of a child not yet able to write . . . she has experienced yachts, jets, helicopters, been whisked through customs, had Secret Service men in attendance almost all her life (with three more years to go under law) . . . already she has participated with the regality of a royal princess in two highly social weddings (those of Janet Auchincloss and Liza Lloyd) . . . she heard Queen Elizabeth dedicate a plot of English soil to the perpetual memory of her father while her mother wept . . . she saw the White House, the Changing of the Guard, Argentina, the Greek Isles, Ireland, Hawaii and Italy before age ten . . . an airplane named for her resides in the Smithsonian . . . her camera came from the Lion of Judah, Emperor Haile Selassie of Ethiopia; her four-foot dollhouse from Madame de Gaulle . . . she once kept a President waiting while she rushed off a heliport to kiss the puppy of a Soviet spacedog . . . she has sat in the Four Seasons with Uncle Stash and been introduced to Orson Welles, Imogene Coca, Jan Sterling and Shirley Booth all at one time . . . she shot the rapids in a kayak with her Uncle Bobby, and has already been to more christenings and funerals than the average adult attends in a lifetime . . . she asked the financial head of Lazard Frères to help her out with the new math (André Mayer, her mother's financial advisor, got six out of the ten problems wrong) . . . she has been skiing at Gstaad, Sun Valley, New England and St. Moritz . . . she has gone backstage after *The Nutcracker* ballet to play in the stage set . . . sat next to idols like Rudolph

Nureyev at tea . . . ridden after foxes and won blue ribbons in the horse ring . . . christened the largest man-of-war ever to sail the seas . . . realized since she was able to know anything much at all that her mother is the best-known woman in the world. . . .

Normal? Not quite. But par for a Kennedy. And she is the Super Kennedy, J.F.K.'s own. . . . Caroline's late grandfather, Joseph P. Kennedy, claimed she was a "genius" and even when she was a tot preferred her company to all others for hours on end.

In her book, *The Kennedy Women*, Pearl S. Buck notes that there have been no leaders among the Bouviers and says that while Jacqueline's children will absorb from her "good taste, the artistic tendencies, the love of beauty so natural to her . . . it is doubtful if they will become leaders." Some think Miss Buck has forgotten the quintessential Kennedy lurking in Jackie's home. Given Caroline's natural qualities of leadership, her brains, her father's heritage, and her bursting good looks, anything could happen in this age of booming Women's Liberation. "I can't imagine Caroline ever becoming a very 'social' person," says one of the Bouviers. "I *can* imagine her becoming the first woman President of the United States."

Set at The Castle Press in Intertype Walbaum,
a light, open typeface designed by
Justus Erich Walbaum (1768-1839),
who was a typefounder at Weimar.
Printed on Hallmark Eggshell Book paper.
Designed by Rainer K. Koenig.